LEY LINES
of the
south west

Alan Neal

Bossiney Books · Launceston

This reprint 2009

First published 2004 by Bossiney Books Ltd
Langore, Launceston, Cornwall PL15 8LD
www.bossineybooks.com

ISBN 978-1-899383-67-2

Cover design by Heards Design Partnership, using photographs
by Paul White. Illustrations on page 30 by Robin Paris

Printed in Great Britain by R Booth Ltd, Penryn, Cornwall

1 A place of enchantment

One day in late June I set off up the path to Cadsonbury (map grid reference SX344674). Clambering over the roadside stile, I paused in the heavy, breathless air to gaze up at the steep slope ahead. It was a familiar route taken many times, treacherous in rain yet unyielding as concrete in both frost and sun.

I climbed slowly, occasionally pausing to look back at the diminishing woodland below, the sound of the river Lynher gradually lessening until it faded to nothing. At last the ground levelled out, and ahead loomed the outline of a gorse-swathed rampart. Up here a slight breeze made a welcome contrast to the oppressive heat of the valley.

Throwing down my rucksack, I stretched out on the soft grass beside the path and surveyed through half-closed eyes two buzzards circling effortlessly high over the hilltop against an infinity of deepest blue. My dog Toby lay curled up beside me. The haunting plaintive cries of the birds became ever more distant as thermals bore them upwards – two tiny dots drifting hypnotically in and out of sight...

With an effort I stirred myself into a state of wakefulness, and grudgingly pulled myself to my feet. Passing through an opening between the ramparts, I was soon standing at the highest point on the central plateau. The view from here was spectactular, out across the undulating greenness to a western horizon dominated by the great bulk of Bodmin Moor: Caradon Hill, Sharp Tor and Stowes Pound, that high prehistoric enclosure (SX257727) topped with its precarious mushroom of boulders nicknamed the Cheesewring.

Cadsonbury is a steep, rounded mass thrusting up incongruously from the Lynher valley like some upturned pudding basin. Long ago its top was levelled off and Iron Age people ringed it round with formidable banks and ditches, turning it into an impressive fortification. Yet to many who have climbed its flanks and wandered along its summit, it has become more than that. With each visit comes a slow realisation that it is imbued with some extra special intangible quality that evades adequate description.

Cadsonbury is not alone in this respect: there are thousands of such 'magical' or 'enchanted' places scattered across the world, and people from all walks of life and belief systems are affected by the noticeably different atmosphere invariably present at each. To attempt to analyse

3

why this is so, it is worth working out what these special places have in common. Probably the most striking characteristic is their power to entice back those who have made only the most fleeting of visits: the desire to return is irresistible. Closely linked to this is a distinct feeling of well-being that can be sensed within a very short time of arrival. To be there raises dulled spirits, at times to the point of ecstasy. So it seems our remote ancestors had good reason to choose these sites for their rituals, ceremonies and perhaps worship – some, such as high hilltops and natural springs, needed no human embellishment, whereas others are entirely man-made and their structural remnants are often still visible today.

But the question still remains: what creates this physical and/or emotional impact on us?

To begin to understand it we must first consider one basic fact. Earth, the planet that is home to us, is far more than a mere mass of rock floating in space. Just as we live, so it lives, and just as our bodies possess a nervous system, so too does the earth. There is nothing new in this philosophy – it forms the basis of the Chinese system of Feng Shui which has been in existence for several thousand years.

The Feng Shui name for the nerves running through earth is 'Ch'i'; our present day Western equivalent is simply 'earth energy'. Other names such as 'pneuma', 'prana' and 'wouivres' have been used in the past and by different cultures.

The exact physical nature of earth energy is beyond the scope of present knowledge, although in some respects it seems to resemble magnetism. A great deal of fanciful speculation has been attached to it, some bordering on the ridiculous, but I am convinced that at some time in the future science will be able to provide a satisfactory explanation. Suffice to say here that we, earth's children and indeed all other living creatures, are inextricably bound to her and can be deeply sensitive to her every nuance.

At certain spots on earth energy lines, namely where they cross one another or, in a similar way to our body's nervous system, where they thicken and form a ganglion from which many smaller lines radiate, the energy is markedly stronger.

Known as 'power centres', these are where dowsers can detect spirals or vortices of energy. Here too a spiritual uplift is often experienced, that enchantment so characteristic of sacred places: stone rows and circles, henges, barrows, holy wells, hillforts – like Cadsonbury – whose true origins and purpose often pre-date the Iron Age, and ancient churches.

Amongst these site types there is another outstanding common phenomenon. The places are often found to be aligned, and these alignments can vary in length from one or two miles to far greater distances. The very frequency with which they occur suggests they are not the result of accident but rather of design. The alignments are known as the Ley System – it is no wonder Cadsonbury is so magical, for passing through it are several ley lines, and many more lines of earth energy cross its summit.

I am able to find leys by dowsing, but for anyone who has not yet acquired this art there is another method of seeking them out, which I shall explain in the next section. (If you'd like to try your hand at dowsing you'll find some tips in chapter 7.)

What is a ley line?

In my work as a dowser I search for the unseen: water, often located deep beneath the earth's surface, walls and foundations of buildings whose whereabouts have been forgotten for years, prehistoric remains whose origins are even older, land drains, broken water pipes, mine workings, lost jewellery… and so the list goes on.

Then there are times when my search carries me into the world of the unknown, to areas which border on the fringes of the mysterious: energies which if not corrected can have an adverse effect on mind and body; footsteps trodden by people long ago, yet to a dowser as clear as if they had walked that way yesterday; presences of those who once lived on earth, yet somehow, often troubled, still remain after death… and then there are ley lines.

As well as practising dowsing on my own, I run elementary and advanced workshops for people to come along and learn 'the Craft'. I can guarantee that the one question I will be asked without fail each time is: 'What is a ley line?'

A quick answer would be that it is a completely straight alignment across the landscape of places of historic and prehistoric importance. But this is seldom sufficient and gives rise to a host of other queries. Over the following pages I hope to elaborate on what is possibly an over-simplistic definition.

How to look for ley lines

Invariably the second question to arise is: 'How do I find a ley line?' Well, first take a look at an Ordnance Survey map, either 1:50 000 scale (1¹/₄ inches to 1 mile) or, better because the detail is finer, 1:25 000 scale (2¹/₂ inches to 1 mile).

In addition to being a record of geographical features, including those made comparatively recently by man, such as roads, railways, canals, reservoirs, airstrips and lines of pylons, maps record places of historic and prehistoric interest: castles, hillforts, henges, Roman villas, burial mounds, stone rows and circles, standing stones, camps, cairns, dolmens, ancient trackways, moats and mounds, monasteries, priories, cathedrals, crosses, holy wells, historic manor houses, chapels and churches. These relics from the past, in combination with certain geographical features, are of real relevance here, for in the search for ley lines both are essential ingredients.

Open up your map and lay it down on a flat surface where you can study it comfortably. Scan it for any of the historical elements mentioned above, and ring them with a pencil. When looking at churches wherever possible try to establish if they were built before the Reformation (Henry VIII's break with the Church of Rome). Although there are a few exceptions to the rule, churches that occur on ley lines tend to have been built before this time. When you have done this, see what you can find from the following list:

> bridging points and fords on rivers, ponds and the highest points of hills, beacon points, sections of dead straight road, cross roads, and places where for no apparent reason roads suddenly change direction.

Mark these with your pencil too. Thirdly, there are names to consider. Look for those containing the following words:

> Merry, Dod, Toot, Tot or Tut, Tump, Moot, Cole, Cold, Tan or St Anne, Bury, Burgh, Ash, Brent and Beacon, as well as Ley in its various forms: Lay, Lee, Lea and Leigh. If your map is of mid-Devon, then look for the name Nymet. This is a Celtic word meaning 'sanctuary', Nemetona being the goddess of the sacred grove, or 'nemeton'. Places bearing the name are always on or near a ley line. Look too for names of colours: Red, White, Blanche, Black, Gold or Golden.

Draw a ring around each of these.

If you stand back and look at the map now, you will probably have a considerable number of pencil rings scattered across its surface (of course if you've chosen a heavily urbanised area, many ancient sites will have been obliterated over the years by building, so the total you find will be much reduced).

The next step is to see how many of these places align on the map. Ley lines usually begin and end at prominent features – often a distinctively shaped high hill or rock outcrop which can be seen from a great distance. Sometimes these 'terminal points' are less distinctive now, belying their past importance. They include holy wells or sacred springs, henges, stone circles and churches, many of which have superseded much earlier pre-Christian structures. Try to find out the name of the saint to whom any church on your line was dedicated, as this may indicate a possible connection with leys. Significant names are: St Michael, St George, St Mary, St Catherine and St Margaret – Christian saints whose attributes correspond with the earlier pagan deities they replaced.

During your search a useful rule to apply is that if a minimum of five (better still six or seven) sites align over a distance of 25 miles (40km), then you have almost certainly found a ley line. The chances of a six-point ley occurring purely by accident are one in two hundred. For a seven-point ley, the odds of this happening are one in one thousand.

There are two ways of checking for alignments. The best, but unfortunately the most damaging to a map, is to use a length of cotton and a drawing pin. (It damages tables too, so make sure you slip a sheet of hardboard or thick card between map and table!) Make a slip-knot in one end of the cotton, and tie this to the pin. Now find a likely prominent feature and stick the pin firmly through its centre. Using this as a pivot, the length of cotton can be turned through a complete circle, accurately revealing any alignments. If you find some, place a ruler along their length and pencil in the line.

If you prefer your maps without holes, then just use the ruler from the central starting point, but make sure that as it turns its end remains in the same position all the time. A transparent plastic ruler is preferable, because if it slips off line it is much easier to replace in its original position than a wooden one.

Having found a ley line on a map, the next step is to go out and search for it on the ground. If you estimate it to start at a high hill, then go to that place and, with the aid of a compass, align your map and look along the line, seeing if you can spot any of the other features that were pencilled in. Provided you are standing at a good enough vantage point, at least some of the objects plotted on the map will be visible, but in addition it might be possible to make out other lesser landmarks which have escaped the attention of the mapmaker.

It is at this stage of the investigation that exciting things can happen, and remote areas can be full of surprises. Features such as ponds are often found on leys. Particularly in the low light of early morning or evening, which throws the smallest irregularities into relief, the outlines of eroded burial mounds or long abandoned roads running across fields will be revealed.

Other pieces of evidence worth looking out for are alignments of field gateways, hedgerows, sunken straight lanes and notches (artificially cut at some time in the past) on hilltops. Referring back to the map, parish boundaries will sometimes also follow the course of a ley.

From your vantage point check how well the features align on the ground, and compare this with your map findings. Now move on to other points, and as before discover whether additional ones come to light, continuing until you have reached the ley's end. This could be considerably beyond where you first anticipated because of other unmapped landmarks.

Unfortunately, it's not always possible to follow a line along its complete course, because it's very unlikely you will find one which runs entirely on common land. But work out where roads cut across the line you have drawn, and go to these places and search for clues.

Also make good use of public footpaths wherever they are marked on the map. If you do feel the need to venture onto private ground, please respect the owner's rights, and always ask their permission first. Quite often they will not only allow you in, but also will show a genuine interest in what you are doing.

How did ley lines get their name?

'Ley' is an Anglo-Saxon word meaning an enclosed field or pasture. It also means a forest clearing, land that is fallow and, in an early form, fire or flame. Alfred Watkins, the man responsible for re-discovering the ley system, first used the name because of the frequency with which it occurs in various forms along alignments.

In his youth Watkins worked in his father's brewing and flour milling business in Hereford as a sales representative, and later in life he rose to the position of senior partner. He was a keen amateur naturalist, a bee keeper and a collector of folklore, much of which he gathered on his journeys around Herefordshire in the course of his work. He was also an accomplished photographer, a Fellow of the Royal Photographic Society and an inventor, devising an exposure meter which enabled photographers for the first time to judge accurately the necessary aperture setting on their cameras. And in public life he served as a county councillor, school governor and magistrate.

The idea that ancient and holy sites are connected by a series of straight lines came to him one day as an inspirational vision while he was sitting in his car looking out over the countryside from a hilltop near the village of Blackwardine. Later, with the aid of maps, he confirmed his vision, and it was then that other details came to light: certain names, including 'Ley' and those I've already mentioned, occurred frequently on alignments, and these often traced the course of prehistoric trackways.

This revelation took place on 30 June 1921. It was no young man's flight of fancy – Watkins was sixty at the time – and neither was it a charlatan's attempt at deception: his honesty was beyond reproach. (Although known to have been psychic, he would never have openly admitted it during his lifetime – public opinion was much less broad-minded then than it is today.) Watkins related his experience to his son, the late Allen Watkins who recalled it in a biography of his father.

For a detailed study of leys, and everything involved in the search for them, I strongly recommend Alfred Watkins's own book *The Old Straight Track*. First published in 1925, it is now once more in print. Neither dated nor dry, it is as fresh, readable and relevant today as when it was first written. I first came across information about place and colour names in this book, and have been able to verify its accuracy time and time again.

I have discovered that all ley lines are dowsable and are just as easy to locate as anything else in a dowser's repertoire. So, if I work out a likely looking alignment on a map, I have only to check it over with my pendulum to ascertain whether or not it is authentic. There will be more information on dowsing later on, but for now the method used for finding ley lines outlined in this chapter is virtually the same, albeit in a slightly less sophisticated form (he used draughtsman's instruments), as that employed by Alfred Watkins

What was the purpose of ley lines?

Of the large number of books describing ley lines, few venture far into questioning the reason for their existence or how they came to be there in the first place.

Alfred Watkins initially believed they served only one purpose: they were tracks used by prehistoric people to make their way across an untamed landscape that was rugged, thickly forested, marshy, and inhabited by wild animals. In effect he believed leys were a type of navigation system.

Later on, as more lines were discovered, it became evident that this could not have been their sole function. Some leys followed the most precipitous ways straight up steep mountainsides or across marshes – hardly practical routes for those travellers and traders in flint, salt and pottery that Watkins had envisaged.

Although some doubtless were purely straight pathways, others were there for different, perhaps more altruistic reasons which combined science, religion and the practicalities of everyday life. Today priest and scientist usually tread very different paths which seldom cross, but in the Bronze Age and before, where most leys have their origins, I believe the priesthood embraced both disciplines.

Lines that were directed towards the point on the horizon where the sun rises at certain times of the year – midsummer, midwinter or the equinoxes – must have been used as a kind of farming almanac, as well as being almost certainly linked to ritual practices.

Others pointing at extreme lunar positions very probably fulfilled the same function. Then there were those which, although joining what must obviously have been prominent places, seem to serve no other purpose than to provide navigable routes for travellers.

A truer picture will often be revealed by looking at a map covering a large area, for it is then that patterns begin to emerge. Some leys run parallel with each other, and some sites, invariably of great prehistoric importance, form the crossing point of several leys (at Cadsonbury, for instance, I counted seven).

Considering them in this greater perspective, it would seem that each one is an integral part of a grand scheme, a work of sophistication almost certainly attributable to those same priestly scientists who sensed that certain sites were very special places. We can only guess at what their beliefs may have been but, judging from the quite spontaneous feelings of inner peace and well-being which so many locations on leys evoke, I like to think they were a deeply spiritual people.

Since the serious study of ley lines began, other suggestions for their possible use have been put forward, including a means of transmitting thoughts via a sort of telepathic telephone service, and a web of healing lines directed into certain areas, bringing with them prosperity and good health. My own belief, which stems from my dowsing experience, is that in their first, most basic form they were used to encourage wild animals into places which had been cleared of trees and where they could be more easily hunted. This method of herding into clearings, which later became enclosed, eventually led to the domestication of animals and to early farms.

One of the most remarkable facts about the ley system is that it is universal. Evidence of it can be found in North and South America, China, Australia, the Middle East, parts of Africa, India… It would seem that over the millennia members of our species shared a common technology, no matter where they happened to be situated.

There are many ley lines to be found in the South West, but limitations of space have restricted me to describing only a few examples. Even though those included fall short of the 25-mile (40 km) used for checking (see page 7), no matter; I have travelled the length of each one, finding adequate reference points and/or verifying their existence through dowsing. Avoiding areas such as West Penwith and Glastonbury, already amply covered by other books, I have deliberately set out to explore some less familar but equally fascinating places. For me the experience was an exhilarating one and I hope that it will inspire you, the reader, to become the explorer. You will find that, as with so many of life's quests, the journey can bring as much fulfilment as its ending, carrying you along hidden byways of beauty and tranquillity.

Unlike buildings, leys can never be destroyed, and as long as we remember how to follow them, they will always be there to point the way and guide us to those places of enchantment once so treasured by our ancestors.

N

Bray Down — North Hill — South Hill — St Dominick — Bere Ferrers

2 From estuary to moor

The Tavy Ley runs for a distance of nearly 20^1/$_2$ miles (32.9 km). From the tidal reaches of the Devon river which gives it its name it climbs steadily until it reaches Bray Down, one of the finest viewpoints in North Cornwall.

The village of **Bere Ferrers** (SX455635) stands to the East of a V-shaped peninsula of land overlooking the River Tavy. At the tip of the V, her waters meet those of her sister, the River Tamar, which forms the boundary between Devon and Cornwall. From here, ever widening, they flow on together to meet the sea at Plymouth.

Travelling in a NE direction from the village, having passed the church and pub, the road runs between the river and an area of marsh. **The ley is first found** about 30 yards (27 m) before reaching a converted chapel on the left-hand side (461635), heading inland 54 degrees NW.

Whilst in Bere Ferrers it's worth stopping a while to explore the 13th-century church with its 14th-century stained glass (some of the oldest in the country), Knight's tomb of the same age, and Elizabethan bench ends. The church was built on the foundations of a much older Saxon church, and looks out onto a wide expanse of river. When I was last there, I stood and watched spellbound as skein after skein of wild geese came honking in to gather on the water in the fading evening light.

The countryside here, now a picture of tranquillity, was once a far busier, more populous place with silver, tin and lead mines, smelting furnaces, lime kilns and, on the sheltered south-facing slopes, market gardening and fruit and flower growing (which still continue today). The rivers too were centres of activity, carrying goods and passengers to and from Plymouth and beyond. In medieval times people could obtain passports from Plymouth, and many travellers set off on their pilgrimage to Santiago de Compostela from the mouth of the Tamar.

Although the line can be traced where it crosses several narrow lanes, there is little else of interest to be seen on the Bere Ferrers peninsula, except where it passes over **a sharp right-angled bend** in the road (432654), a feature commonly found on leys.

Not directly on it, but nearby to the north is Ley Farm (452646). Coincidence? Perhaps. In Saxon times it was a manor known as Legh, but just to confuse the issue it was bought by Sir James Ley, who later became the Earl of Marlborough during the reign of James I.

The next ley point to be found is on the western bank of the River Tamar. Unfortunately there is no bridging point, the nearest one being at Gunnislake, so this necessitates a long roundabout drive to the place where the line crosses the lane between **Halton Quay and St Dominick** (415667). It was near to Halton Quay that St Indract and his sister St Dominica, the children of a king, are reputed to have come in AD 689, having voyaged from Ireland (the parish church of nearby St Dominick was dedicated to St Dominica). A chapel marks the entrance to the creek where they landed, although the creek itself is now blocked off by the quay. Redundant lime kilns stand nearby; signs of busier days when a ferry plied between here and the Devonshire bank opposite.

St Dominick church (399678) stands on a steeply sloping hillside, sheltered by huge beech trees. The Tavy Ley passes diagonally through it, encompassing the whole building, except for a small section of the tower. Parts of the original structure, dedicated in October 1259 by the Bishop of Exeter, Walter de Bronescombe, still exist: the north wall, the east wall of the chancel and the lower part of the tower.

Look at the stonework just below the parapet. There on three sides – south, east and west – you will see figures of what are thought to be nine of the twelve apostles. Inside the church there is a fine barrel-vaulted roof with carved bosses, and the 17th-century tomb of Sir Anthony Rous, one time High Sheriff of Cornwall, and of his son Ambrose.

On leaving St Dominick, the ley follows a straight stretch of road before heading off into the fields at a **T junction** (397680). Passing close to, but not touching **Dupath Holy Well** (375693), it runs to the NE of Callington, crossing the **A390** (370698) **and the A3257** (360705). Dominating the landscape to the NE is Kit Hill, 1091 feet (333 metres) high, with its distinctive chimney-shaped obelisk. NE of Callington, the line cuts directly through the centre of a **Y junction**

(353712), and follows another straight stretch of road almost as far as **Maders** (346716).

At the centre of a small group of houses that is the hamlet of **South Hill**, to the NE of a crossroads, stands its **church** (329727), through which the ley next passes. Consecrated in 1333, much of the original building remains intact, but its cruciform shape has undergone medieval alteration. This is the mother church of nearby Callington, dedicated to St Samson (or Sampson), who came over from South Wales in the 6th century.

From South Hill the Tavy Ley heads off towards **Linkinhorne village** (318736) and, although not touching either, it passes directly between Linkinhorne church and Holy Well, close to a **T junction** (318735). Both are dedicated to St Melor (or Mylor), thought to have been the early Breton abbot-bishop, Saint Meloir, and repay a visit. The well, situated in a marshy valley, is not easy to find. It is housed in a small granite building of a type typical to Cornwall, with steeply pitched roof and arched entrance. It has a lovely atmosphere all of its own.

From Linkinhorne, the ley carries on for a distance of some 2½ miles (4 km), crossing four small lanes before coming to a **cross roads** (286757).

At some places on ley lines the immediate feeling of sanctity comes as no great surprise: an old church, such as the ones I've described here, a standing stone, a holy well – these major sites venerated for centuries must surely harbour and emanate strong traces of that reverence. But in other places, which ostensibly have no known significance, the sense that they are nonetheless special sometimes dawns on you so quietly that it isn't until after leaving when the full realisation hits home. With the ley passing directly through its centre, this cross roads was just such a place. When I was last there, only one tractor passed by in the space of half an hour to disturb the silence, and in hindsight I realise I felt complete peace and well-being.

The ley next crosses the **B3254** (277765) before entering **North Hill**, a granite village sheltering beneath the rugged mass of Bodmin Moor. Just as at St Dominick and South Hill, it passes diagonally through the **church** (272766). This is dedicated to St Torney (or Terney) whose name appears in corrupted form in another Cornish parish, that of St Erney. Almost all of the existing building, with its high graceful tower, dates from the 15th century. However, as the first incumbent is on record as having been at St Torney in 1260, it is very likely that there was an earlier church on the site.

From the church the Tavy Ley follows a straight section of road until it disappears through the gates of **Trebartha Estate** (264773). It re-emerges to cut across a **narrow lane** (255779) leading to North Bowda and Basstreet. From here it follows the rim of the wild, rock-strewn moor, its lower slopes softened by woodland that in autumn is transformed to gold.

After crossing the **A30 SW of Trewint** (218804), the ley climbs onto higher, more rugged ground, past Trewint Downs, Carne Down, with its hut circles, and on to **Bray Down** (189823), standing at 1135 feet (346 metres).

The route leading up Bray Down from Bowithick is not a smooth one, and while picking my way through a confusion of rocks, bracken and moorgrass I followed the well trodden tracks of sheep and cattle. At the summit a cool breeze was wafting in from the Atlantic, despite it being a summer's day. All around lay a scatter of cairns, some still recognisable, some reduced to almost nothing. Here were the last remnants of a Bronze Age people who could work metal, who were farmers, whose stone rows and circles showed a knowledge of sophisticated geometry and astronomy, and who, I believe, engineered and utilised the system of ley lines we can still find today.

Starting at its south-eastern end, and gradually working my way north-westwards, I traversed the hilltop, searching for the ley with my dowsing rods. With each traverse there it was, travelling just as it had been at Bere Ferrers: 54 degrees NW. Then, after passing the most northerly cairn which is the largest and has a natural rock outcrop at its centre, it stopped... Time and again I searched beyond this point, but there was nothing. The Tavy Ley ended here.

For a while I stood at the top of the cairn, taking in the panoramic view: the jagged tors of Bodmin Moor, Kit Hill, Caradon Hill, the great undulating mass of Dartmoor, and far in the distance the dim dark outline of Exmoor. Away to the north east was the sea, glittering in the afternoon sunlight, and within it the green outline of Lundy Island. It is, I thought, no small wonder that people of long ago considered this to be a place of such importance.

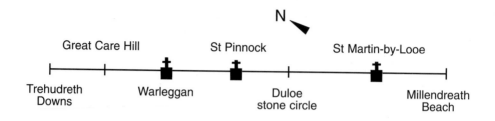

Great Care Hill   St Pinnock   St Martin-by-Looe

Trehudreth
Downs   Warleggan   Duloe
stone circle   Millendreath
Beach

3 The St Martin Ley

Running between a small bay on the south-east coast of Cornwall, a short distance from the town of Looe and the high downland of Bodmin Moor, the St Martin Ley takes its name from the church of St Martin-by-Looe through which it runs. It is just over 14 1/2 miles (23 km) long.

The narrow road leading to **Millendreath Beach** (SX 268541) winds steeply down through the trees from the B3253 that runs between Looe and Widegates. On the day of my visit a few last holiday-makers lay sunning themselves in the late August sunlight and a flat lazy sea lapped at the grey shore. Leaving my car, I walked down to the water's edge and followed the shoreline westwards.

My rods soon picked out the spot where the St Martin Ley first made landfall, heading inland in the direction of 330° NNW. I followed it as far as I could, but soon came to a halt at the back of the narrow beach where the upper windows of a house peeped unhappily down at me over the rim of a crumbly looking cliff. Unable to search any further here, I returned to the car and drove back up the valley, heading for the next point on the ley.

The **church of St Martin-by-Looe** (259551) lies beneath the brow of the hill, almost hidden from the view of anyone passing by on the B3253. Walking along the churchyard path on its southern side, I once more came upon the line where it headed towards the building, before passing through it diagonally.

St Martin was a 4th-century Bishop of Tours who, whilst serving in the Roman Army, apparently cut his cloak in half and gave one part to a beggar on a cold winter's day. Although the church now bears his name, it was originally dedicated to St Kayne, one of those Celtic

Christian missionaries who came to Cornwall in the 5th or 6th century. She was a princess, one of fifteen daughters of a Welsh king.

It is thought that long before 1258, when the present church was dedicated, a place of worship stood here, and perhaps it was on this very spot that St Kayne set up her oratory.

Nestling among the trees beneath the hilltop and at a distance from the centre of the population it serves, it is typical of the places chosen by these hermit-evangelists. The fact that a ley passes directly through it gives added credence to this theory, and as is so often the case could indicate the presence of a much earlier, pre-Christian place of worship of some importance.

Little remains of the fabric of the original church, except for a Norman north door, and a 13th-century lancet in the south wall near the tower, now containing a stained glass image of St Martin. Much of the stonework to be seen today is 14th and 15th century.

After leaving St Martin's, the ley crosses the **A387** (249564) near Sandplace. It goes on to pass close to **St Cuby's Holy Well** (241579), then on over the hill to the **Duloe stone circle** (236584). This is best reached by parking outside the **church** (234582), and walking down the B3254 towards the village. After a right-hand bend, you will see a stone cottage and a barn on the right, and between them a small lane marked 'Pedestrians Only'. Follow this lane until you come to a gate. Go through the gate, and the circle is ahead, on the opposite side of the field.

The most striking feature of the Duloe stone circle is the quartz-rich rock from which it is made, containing the mineral ankerite. This gives it a whitish-grey colouring which is very different from the darker granite found in most prehistoric Cornish monuments.

Small the circle may be, but this is amply compensated for by the sheer size of each stone. Seven of these are upright and one has fallen. Dating from the Bronze Age, probably some time between 2200 and 1500 BC, it is not really circular, but ovoid in shape.

Restoration work by the Reverend T A Bewes of Plymouth between 1858 and 1861, in which a bisecting hedge was removed and fallen stones were re-erected, resulted in the largest stone being broken, and it still lies recumbent. At its base was found an urn containing human remains, but unfortunately the urn and its contents crumbled to dust when exposed to the air.

As it passes along the ridge above Duloe village, the St Martin Ley encompasses the whole stone circle, then crosses the **B3254 near Polvean Cross** (234586) before heading off towards **Black Down** (224599) (a name frequently found on leys) and passing close to its summit. From here, after travelling some 2½ miles (4 km), it reaches the small hamlet of **St Pinnock**, passing through its **church** (201632).

Little is known of the origins of St Pinnock (real name probably Pynnocus), but the church, originally cruciform, could well stand on the site of his oratory. As in so many ancient churches, scars left by the Victorian 'restorers' are all too evident: black and yellow tiles on the floor, pitchpine pews, lack of old glass... Luckily the Norman font, with carved heads, an early piscina and some original roof bosses and plates still remain, and the 15th-century granite pillars are unscathed.

Past St Pinnock, the ley heads NNW at 330°, crossing the **A390** (193643) and the **B3360** (191645) at the very top of the hill where **the road suddenly changes direction**.

Descending to the Glynn Valley, it crosses the A38 at **Two Waters Foot** (188649), near to the point where the Fowey and St Neot rivers meet. Climbing the farther slope, it passes close to the small settlement of **Ley** (177664) at a sharp bend in the road, then over a cross roads on **Goonzion Down** (174668) from where it heads for the moorland church of **Warleggan** (157692).

Warleggan village has been described by various writers as 'lonely', 'remote', 'desolate and almost deserted'. Perhaps now with the busy A30 and A38 roads not so far away, and close proximity to the extensive and popular Colliford Lake reservoir, these descriptions have lost a little of their edge, but it is worth remembering that mains electricity never reached Warleggan until 1965.

Warleggan church is approached by a small secluded cul-de-sac shaded by tall sycamore trees. Standing on a hilltop, it has a circular churchyard, two factors which, as the guidebook says, indicate an ancient burial site. Additional weight is added to this argument by the presence of the St Martin Ley passing right through the church.

Compared with St Martin's and St Pinnock, St Bartholomew at Warleggan appears small and squat, a fitting refuge from the biting winds which cut across the moor in winter. But in common with St Pinnock there is ample evidence of Victorian restoration, including pitchpine roof-boards and pews. Little remains of the pre-Victorian fabric, except for a 15th-century font, an 18th-century poor-box, and the Royal Arms of 1664, given in acknowledgement of the parish's loyalty to Charles I during the Civil War. To the left of the south door is a weathered Celtic cross, probably 8th century and moved there from the moorland path which leads to nearby Temple church.

It is unclear when Warleggan church, probably built initially as a manorial chapel, was first dedicated – there is evidence of a Rector, John Wak, being there in 1244. In more recent times the incumbency of the Reverend F W Densham, Rector from 1931 to 1953, has attracted most attention. Because of his very fixed views and somewhat autocratic nature, Reverend Densham fell out with the Parochial Church Council. Over the years the rift widened, his eccentricities increased and he became a recluse with only his dogs for company. Because people stopped attending his church services, it is rumoured that he placed cut-out cardboard figures in the pews as a substitute congregation.

This sad tale of loneliness drew to a close when one day his body was found on the stairs of his rectory, where he had died alone. On my way out of the church, I noticed a small wooden door in the wall of the rectory grounds, and I felt a pang of sorrow for the solitary old man who must have emerged from it so many times to offer up prayers in an empty house of worship.

From Warleggan the St Martin Ley heads off towards Cardinham Moor, crossing **Great Care Hill** (142713) a little to the SW of its summit. Even when not following a ley, this place is rewarding to visit because of the views over the little village of Temple (famous for its connections with the Knights Templar) and the moorland expanse higher up, with its rugged outlines of Roughtor, Brown Willy and, to the north east, far off Kilmar Tor. (If you decide to walk on the Great Care area of the moor, always ensure there are no red warning flags flying, as the area is close to the Millpool firing range.)

From Great Care Hill the ley descends into a marshy hollow, then climbs again towards the busy A30 where it runs across Trehudreth Downs. I followed the fenceline taking note of two distinctive hawthorn trees growing near the point where it **crosses the road** (132725) a short distance SW of the turning to Temple.

Looking at the fast flow of unyielding traffic, I decided it best to approach the higher part of **Trehudreth Downs** (128728) from the opposite side of the A30. I parked my car at Manor Common (135740), and walked up, heading for two cairns at the summit. But these were not on the ley, and I made my way back to the road, this time on its northern side.

Beside the fence, a thicket of high grass and brambles muffled the continuous tumult of traffic. While a group of cows with young calves eyed us suspiciously, I searched along the fenceline. Toby wisely stayed beside me as we passed them by. Soon my left rod began twitching, and then gradually both left and right came together, parallel with each other. Peering over the undergrowth, I could just make out the tops of my two hawthorn markers on the far side of the road, and I knew with certainty that this was the right place.

Turning to my right, I followed the ley in a north-westerly direction. It appeared to be running just to the SW of the cairns which top Trehudreth Downs. Walking up the gently sloping hillside I seemed to be entering another world far from the hubbub of civilisation. Weather-bleached bones of a long-dead sheep lay scattered around a gorse bush where foxes and ravens had left them, and from a patch of marshy ground a snipe darted swiftly into the air.

Ahead of me, a little to my left, three standing stones loomed up on the skyline, and just beyond them the almost obliterated remains of what had once been a large cairn, most of its stones robbed long ago, probably for walling. It was a desolate, lonely place, yet its solitude came as a soothing balm after the frenzied bustle of the busy road, so near and yet worlds away.

As I neared the highest point of the downs I noticed that, instead of pointing ahead, my rods began swinging backwards towards me every now and again. This is what I call the 'Behind me' signal, meaning that I have passed over whatever I'm looking for. The St Martin line I had been following for over 14 miles (22 km) was slowly fading, unlike the Tavy line which finished so abruptly on Bray Down. Presently there was no reaction at all.

To the people who came to the downs and created a meaningful site at the ley's ending, this must once have been a revered and cherished place, perhaps visited by many for rituals that are long since forgotten; but now my only company was a dog at my feet, a nearby group of curious-eyed ponies, and the relentless, buffeting upland wind.

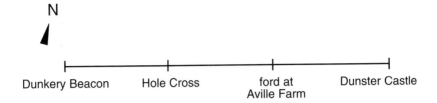

4 The Dunster Ley, Somerset

As I took the last few steps of the rough stone track and climbed the cairn that stands at the highest point of **Dunkery Beacon** (SS 892416), a flurry of sleet came sweeping in from the Severn Sea on a wet, icy wind. This was the winter face of Exmoor, that high, wild country stretching eastwards from Barnstaple Bay in Devon across north Somerset, almost as far as the Quantock Hills. How different it had been a few short months ago, clad in a glory of purple heather, the air clear and still.

A little ahead of me lay the eroded remains of two more cairns, their bare stones glistening in the damp air. Moving from north to south I paced the ground in front of them, searching with my rods. The points began to move together, and I knew I had found what I was looking for: the high point of the Dunster Ley, running ENE from Dunkery Beacon to Dunster Castle, a distance of 8 1/4 miles (13.3 km). For a short moment the grey murk cleared, and across the water I caught a glimpse of the coast of Wales and in the distance the dim dark outline of the Brecon Beacons; then, once more they vanished and the rain came scudding in.

Heading north, I came to the A39 at **Brandish Street** (906467), and turning right drove eastwards for 1 3/4 miles (3 km) before turning right at **Venniford Cross** (931458) to **Wootton Courtenay**. This is hilly, wooded country, dotted with honey-coloured cottages, sitting round and comfortable beneath their covering of thatch.

Turning right at the village Post Office and then taking a right fork (marked as a no-through-road), I stopped at **Hole Cross** (933424), a few yards on from the gate to Stile Farm. The ley was here, coming to the Cross from the south west along an old sunken track nestling deep beneath tree-lined banks, its ruts awash with flowing muddy water. Now seldom used, except by occasional farm traffic, this place felt as though it had been of some importance in the past. Surely nobody would have bothered to excavate its course so deeply had not some special purpose been in mind.

Re-tracing my route back to Wootton Courtenay, I turned right, driving on to **Cowbridge Cross** (956431) where I took a right turn. After around 330 yards (300 m), the Dunster line crossed the road at **Timberscombe Cricket Club** (956427), just before Cow Bridge.

Returning to Cowbridge Cross and turning right again, I followed Knowle Lane that runs along the valley of the River Avill. Close by is the course taken by the Dunster line. It crosses the bridleway leading to **Aville Farm** very close to a **footbridge and ford** (976433), about 100 yards (90 m) from the road. (Fords, bridges and crossroads are all commonly found on leys.)

Soon Knowle Lane joins the A396 near **Frackford Bridge** (985433), running into **Dunster** where the magnificent **castle** (992434) set on a high mound above the village dominates the scene.

We know that a castle was built here in the 11th century by its Norman owner, William de Mohun, and that before the Conquest it was a fortified site occupied by the Saxon Aelfric; but I believe that because of its situation, commanding an important north-south trade route, it was originally an Iron Age hillfort – as were nearby Bat's Castle and Gallax Hill.

The castle passed to the Luttrell family in 1376, and eighteen generations lived there until 1976 when its ownership was transferred to The National Trust. Much of what we see of it today is a Victorian, medieval-style reconstruction by the architect Anthony Salvin, who was employed by George Fownes Luttrell in the late 1860s.

Walking through Dunster, past the famous 16th-century Yarn Market and the Priory Church of St George, I finally came upon the Dunster Ley. It crossed Mill Lane and headed straight towards its terminal point, the upper ward of the castle on the top of the tor.

Here at the very seat of power, it ended.

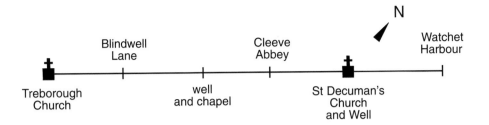

5 The Watchet Ley, Somerset

Some 6 miles (10 km) along the coast to the east of the busy holiday town of Minehead lies the ancient port of **Watchet**. Nowadays yachts and other pleasure craft are moored here, but there was a time when commercial industry thrived – woollen cloth was exported, and South Wales coal was imported from across the Bristol Channel.

Near to the harbour wall is a bronze statue of the Ancient Mariner who in the poem of the same name by Samuel Taylor Coleridge foolishly shot an albatross, bringing disaster upon himself and his shipmates. Coleridge lived for some years at nearby Nether Stowey and visited the town in 1797 whilst on a walking tour. It is said that the view of the harbour inspired him to write his poem.

Swain Street runs northwards towards the harbour, and just before the slipway it makes a 90° turn to the west, where it meets Market Street. It is on this **sharp bend** (ST 071435) that the Watchet Ley will first be found, coming in from the sea between western and eastern piers.

Twenty-four paces wide, it travels SW for 5 3/4 miles (9.25 km) to the church of Treborough, high on a ridge of the Brendon Hills. Leaving Watchet on the B3190, after about half a mile (800 m), I took a **right turn** (066426), heading towards **St Decuman's church** whose tower can clearly be seen a short distance from the road. Standing where it does, on a hill overlooking the sea, this seems a fitting place for a church serving a port, the port to which St Decuman, a Celtic monk, came from Rhoscrowther in South Wales in the 6th century.

The Watchet line passes through the main body of the building, which was developed from an earlier 13th century structure. It has a wagon roof and beautifully carved screens, and it stands on what is probably one of the oldest Christian sites in west Somerset.

(Follow the road that runs downhill to the north of the church, and within a very short distance you'll find St Decuman's Well. This shrine's origins go back long before the days of Christianity. It is one of the most beautifully kept places of its kind I have come across – the carefully laid out garden is sheltered by mature trees and the constant murmur of flowing water enhances an atmosphere comparable only with that found at Glastonbury's Chalice Well.)

Leaving St Decuman's, the line crosses the A39 main road at **Lower Washford** (052411) before reaching **Cleeve Abbey** (047407) where it passes diagonally through the gatehouse. Run by the Cistercian Order, the Abbey was founded during the 12th century by William de Roumare, Earl of Lincoln. Unlike so many buildings of its kind which were completely destroyed after the Dissolution of the Monasteries in 1536, a large part of Cleeve has been preserved, more as a result of good fortune than design.

In the 16th century it was turned into a private house before being used as a farm. The buildings remained intact and were kept roofed instead of being used as a convenient stone quarry. The Chapter House, cloisters and even some original wall decorations have survived to give us a clearer idea of how life must have been for the Cistercians. Sadly, the Abbey Church did not escape the attention of the King's henchmen, who, as was the custom at the time, did all they could to erase any evidence of its former existence.

Continuing along its south-westerly course, the ley follows the side of the valley, passing very close to a **well and chapel** (042398) on the left-hand side of the road, just before Roughmoor Copse. This is St Pancras (known locally as 'St Prankett's') Well.

Although marked on the map, there would appear to be no current signed access. The chapel is 13th century, and is thought to have been originally a hermit's cell built next to a spring. After the Reformation it was converted into a cottage, and has remained so ever since.

Passing through Lower Roadwater and Roadwater, after about 1¾ miles (2.8km), to the north of Glasses Farm, the line then runs through two typical ley points. First, it crosses the end of **Blindwell Lane** (026382), a name signifying the probable existence of a healing well or spring in the vicinity; then it crosses a ford.

In this area there is a proliferation of springs emerging from the steep hillsides. Although not 'wells' in the generally accepted sense, that is holes dug above underground watercourses, it is the title that they have been given.

To follow the final 1¼ miles (2km) of the Watchet Ley, I turned near Glasses Farm, heading back the way I'd come, then took the **first right turn** (028379) for **Treborough** (011364), a small hamlet consisting of a few cottages and a farm. As I came to some crossroads the light was starting to fade, and I could just make out the outline of the church tower in the gathering darkness.

Although threequarters rebuilt in the 19th century, Treborough Church was originally constructed some time between 1291 and 1320 (there are records of a vicar being instituted in 1321).

I knew that at this late hour the church would be locked, but entering the churchyard I walked along the north wall of the building, searching for the Watchet line – and there it was, still twenty-four paces wide, at the end of its journey from the Severn sea to this small ancient church high on the Brendon Hills.

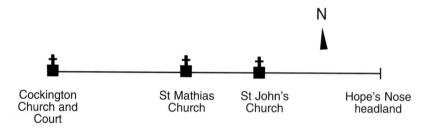

N

| Cockington Church and Court | St Mathias Church | St John's Church | Hope's Nose headland |

6 The Cockington Ley

Found entirely by dowsing, the Cockington Ley comes in from the sea from the direction of the **Lead Stone** (SX 952635), a large outcrop of rock off **Hope's Nose** headland, Torquay. For much of its course it runs through the town whose proliferation over the years must have obliterated many of the reference points marking its course.

Emerging into the countryside just outside the suburb of Chelston, it ends at the picturesque village of Cockington, around 3¹/₂ miles (5.6 km) from its starting point.

Torbay is a busy place in July, so to avoid the inevitable traffic I arrived at seven o'clock one Sunday morning. As I parked my car in Ilsham Marine Drive the air was warm and still, promising a hot summer's day. Far below me, a flat, almost motionless sea reflected the deep blue of the sky, and the normally grey Leadstone and Orestone rocks gleamed white in the early sunlight. I knew that the line I was looking for could not be far away, having found it on the map some days beforehand.

Beginning at the **road junction** (945635), I began walking south, searching with my rods. Within a few yards, they reacted, indicating to me that I was in the right place. A compass bearing showed that the ley was coming in across the flat rocky promontory of Hope's Nose from the direction of ESE.

I drove west in the direction of Meadfoot Beach, then turning inland up Ilsham Valley, I located the ley again where it **crossed the road** (936635) below Lincombe Slopes. At the head of this valley is Wellswood and the famous Kent's Cavern (renowned for its Palaeolithic remains).

Heading on towards the centre of the town, I parked opposite the **museum** (923636). Beside the road there is a public garden area, and here I continued my search, attracting inquisitive looks from several elderly people. Their curiosity was greatly increased as I crossed over the ley and my rods mysteriously swung together in unison.

The Cockington Ley just skirts the edge of **St John's Church** (919636), standing on a hill above the harbour, and then continues on to where it crosses the northern corner of **Abbey Sands** (913636), between the Rock Walk and the Palm Court Hotel.

Behind Abbey Sands, lawns sweep gently up to a large mansion, Torre Abbey. Until the Reformation this was a monastic house – it was established in the 12th century by the Premonstratensian Order (founded in France by St Norbert in 1120, and known as the white Canons from the colour of the monks' habits). The Abbey was later turned into a private house, and remained as such until it was sold by the Cary family to the Local Authority in the 1930s.

Parts of the original building that still survive include the guest hall, the gatehouse and the great barn, known in the reign of Elizabeth I as the Spanish Barn. Sir George Cary and Sir John Gilbert of nearby Compton Castle held four hundred prisoners here from the *Nuestra Señora del Rosario*, a captured ship from the defeated Armada.

I discovered that the ley passes close to the **south wall of the barn** (907637). From there it crosses two busy main roads north of Torquay Station, heading towards Chelston where it can be found just east of the **railway bridge** (905637).

At the top of Chelston there is a V junction with **St Mathias Church** (901637) at its centre. The ley passes directly along the east-west axis of the building, and can be traced through a large grassy area behind.

Cockington village (895637) is always a mecca for visitors, and this hot July morning was no exception. But it was good to be away from the town traffic and to continue the rest of the journey on foot.

Showpiece though the village may have become, for me it brings back happy childhood memories of walking along country lanes from nearby Shiphay; of a blacksmith's shop where horseshoes were made; and of a weaver's cottage, now silent, where a Scotsman and his wife once worked amid the busy rattle of looms.

The Drum Inn, designed by Sir Edwin Lutyens, whose other work includes Castle Drogo, Liverpool Cathedral and the Whitehall

Cenotaph, at least remains unchanged beneath its covering of thatch. Only completed in 1936, it gives an impression of having been there forever, a part of the landscape.

Cockington Court, together with the **parish church of St George and St Mary** (891637) a short distance from it, lie among verdant parkland at the head of the valley above the village. As I walked up the grassy slope I could easily locate the ley, heading straight towards the church. Pathways and lawns were dotted with people out to enjoy the summer weather, and as it neared eleven o'clock the church bells started to ring.

Approaching the building, the ley was wide, wider than the church itself; but as I drew near to the east wall, it tapered inwards until it was just wide enough to be accommodated within the structure. This is an unusual feature. Leys often remain unchanged by buildings, passing through them whilst retaining their full width.

By now the service was in progress, so I was unable to dowse inside. Instead, I searched around the building for traces of the ley emerging from its west end. Pacing the area behind the tower, I could find no trace of it, although another line, approaching from the ENE (more scope here for future research!), passes right through, undiminished in size. Climbing steps to an area of garden above, I searched twice more for the Cockington Ley, but to no avail. Here within the walls of the church, it ended.

Although the oldest part of the building that we see today is the tower, erected between 1201 and 1250, it is fairly certain a chapel would have existed on the site in Saxon times when the manor was owned by the wealthy thane Alric. But the presence of two leys meeting here would point very strongly to the origins of this sacred place going far back into the depths of time.

7 Finding leys by dowsing

In chapter 1, I mentioned Alfred Watkins and his method of discovering leys on a map: finding sites of historic and prehistoric interest, and seeing if they aligned. I also wrote about his requirements for proof of a ley's existence: the alignment of at least five sites along a twenty-five mile (40 km) stretch. But in searching for leys using dowsing (and I frequently do) none of these requirements is really necessary; in fact some leys crossing the landscape join very few ancient sites, but nonetheless they are very much there, and they are very real.

In the modern world where so many remains of the past have been obliterated by housing, roads and industry, it would be very easy to miss some leys altogether were we to rely purely on Alfred Watkins's methods of search – many of the reference points he would have used have vanished forever.

So, I suggest the best way to begin dowsing for leys is to practise on a line whose existence has been established using the conventional map method. Go to the area in question, and practise on the ground. The fact that you know full well the ley is there in the first place doesn't matter at all. The important part of the lesson is that you are training your mind to 'tune in' to the idea 'ley'. The mind is an instrument and, like all instruments, needs calibrating in order to work accurately.

Practise as much as you can on as many leys as possible. Once you feel reasonably proficient, get a friend to do a map search without telling you exactly what has been found. Then go to the area yourself, undertake your own dowsing search and return to compare results.

Searching for a ley is no more complicated than searching for underground water – something most of us can find fairly easily. Remember that most places that were of importance, particularly in prehistory, will have at least one and sometimes more ley lines in the near vicinity.

The ability to dowse is something I firmly believe is within all of us. As well as the five senses we use in our everyday lives, we have a sixth sense – intuition. Many people are taught to believe only in that which can be seen, and to reject all else. I feel that it is because of this misguided philosophy that intuition is so often ignored or relegated to some backwater of the mind. For too long it has remained dormant, but with dowsing it can be reawakened and brought to the fore to serve us well.

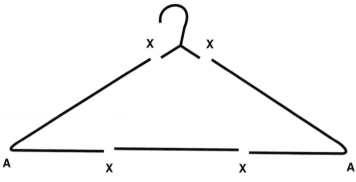

Fig. 1 Making 'L' rods

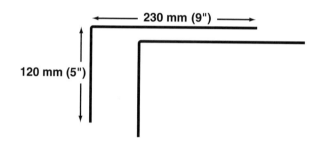

230 mm (9")

120 mm (5")

Fig. 2 Completed 'L' rods

For some years I have been running dowsing courses. At the start of each one I always make a point of telling my students that I'm not going to teach them to dowse, but what I can do is to *show* them that they already possess the innate ability to do it themselves. Once they accept this, we can go on together to develop what is an entirely natural and very useful art.

Making your own dowsing tools

You can make these very easily with wire – a metal coat-hanger is excellent for the job (see fig. 1). Although nowadays not as readily available as their more modern plastic counterparts, it is possible to find them in charity shops.

To save yourself extra work, use the bends (A) already in the hanger, and with a sharp pair of pliers cut where indicated (X). With a little more bending before long you should have your dowsing rods (see fig. 2). The measurements in the diagram are those which, after a lot of trial and error, I have found give the best degree of balance and sensitivity.

In time you may find you need heavier gauge wire to counteract the effect of strong wind, but to start with, given fair weather, your adapted coat-hanger will be adequate.

Now decide what you are searching for, and concentrate on that one item. But don't concentrate too hard. Remember that a dowser's greatest asset is a relaxed state of mind. The greatest disadvantage is anxiety, bringing with it tension and consequent loss of accuracy.

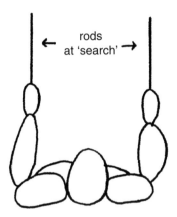

Fig. 3   Holding the rods in the search position

With a clear idea of the object of your search fixed in your mind, point the rods straight ahead of you, held about 16 inches (40 cm) apart, with the points slightly dipped (see fig. 3), and start walking forwards. Let's suppose you are looking for an underground watercourse. As you approach it, you will see the points of the rods coming together and crossing. If you are new to dowsing, this will be your 'found' position. Later, as you progress, the rods will go past the crossover point until they are parallel to each other (see fig. 4). This is the 'found' position for the experienced dowser.

You are now directly above the target of your search. If you carry on walking, the rods will turn inwards towards your body. When this happens, it means you have overshot your target. Step slowly backwards until they are once again parallel.

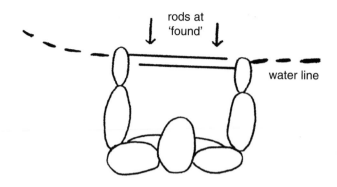

rods at
'found'

water line

Fig. 4 Found position for the experienced dowser

You may find that instead of being parallel to each other in the 'found' position your rods turn outwards, forming a straight line. Don't panic! As individuals we all differ slightly in many ways, and this is just one of them; so for you, this could be 'found'.

Practise with the L rods. They are an uncomplicated and accurate tool that will help you to build up confidence before you move on to other dowsing instruments, such as the pendulum. For further information on dowsing, see my book *Dowsing in Devon and Cornwall* (Bossiney Books 2001).

Bibliography

The old straight track, Alfred Watkins (Abacus)
The dance of the dragon, Hamish Miller & Paul Broadhurst (Pendragon)
The sun and the serpent, Hamish Miller & Paul Broadhurst (Pendragon)
Mysterious Britain, Colin and Janet Bord (Paladin)
Earth magic, Francis Hitching (Picador)
The elements of earth mysteries, Philip Heselton (Element)
Cornovia, Craig Weatherhill (Cornwall Books)
Cornish place names and language, Craig Weatherhill (Sigma)
Prehistoric Cornwall, John Barnalt (Turnstone Press)
The saints of Cornwall, Catherine Rachel John (Tabb House)

For further information on dowsing, contact The British Society of Dowsers, 2 St Ann's Road, Malvern, Worcestershire, WR14 4RG (www.britishdowsers.org).